Friends & Lovers

Friends & Lovers

Walter Rinder

CELESTIAL ARTS
Millbrae, California

Copyright © 1978 by Walter Rinder

CELESTIAL ARTS
231 Adrian Road
Millbrae, California 94030

First Printing, August 1978
Made in the United States of America

Library of Congress Cataloging in Publication Data

Rinder, Walter
      Friends and lovers.

      I. Title.
PS3568.I5F7   811'.5'4   78-54474
ISBN 0-89087-223-6

  2 3 4 5 6 7 — 83 82 81 80 79 78

Introduction

Sharing intimately while building our lives is the most important consideration for a balanced, happy existence. Deep, meaningful friendships are vital — both those that are temporarily filling needs and desires at certain times in our lives and permanent ones that grow and strengthen over many years. They offer us security throughout the changing aspects of ourselves and the extreme acceleration of the world we live in.

There are special friendships each person requires to bring the pieces of their existence together into a wholeness, that offers stability in an otherwise unstable world. One unique friendship is commonly referred to as "being in love" or "lovers" — any two people who devote and commit most of themselves to each other. This type of togetherness is the strongest attraction for people living together, building a home environment, a family, a way of life and a sanctuary for their fantasies, hopes and dreams.

What is clear is that relationships develop through their own nurturing, the desire of individuals to know and share with each other. It will not matter what others may think. What does matter to friends is the caring and respect they have for each other . . . and a friendship that may flourish and deepen into love—a love sanctioned by the Supreme Force of all creation, whatever you may call this Divine Spirit.

The pages that follow are a personal chronicle of my journey into friendship and being in love. . .

Walter Rinder

Dedication
To Doug, whose friendship helped me
complete this book.

I must go a-wandering to find the answers
loving can bring

Hello

You entered my life during a journey which
had taken me thousands of miles from home. I
had been trying to catch up with the sun which
finally led me to your town. I infiltrated your
environment alone, and without commitments.
Our first meeting was brief, yet you stood out
like the moon among the stars. Feelings erupted
within me as your eyes spoke directly of your
gentleness. Your excitement toward life filled my
then tired spirit with renewed stimulation.

As our first meeting ended, after a time of
barest conversation, we both felt an urgent desire
to come together again. We could not leave the
beginnings isolated, for the possibility of
companionship was obvious.

When again we met and spent the evening
together, every moment became precious and we
burst forth with our emotions, our thoughts,
realizing a friendship was beginning and anything
was possible...for us!

I looked into the troubled eyes
of your exhausted face,
a face growing old too soon.
I saw there needs that had
never been fulfilled.
Others had been blind to,
perhaps had even ignored,
those needs.
So I extended my hand,
offering you my friendship
without obligation,
without reservation,
without demands.

You took me to your special place
      in the mountains
      above your town:
I listened intently as you told me
      of its meaning to you during childhood
years
      and of the quiet stream where the limbs of
trees
      stretched far over the water . . .
      the spot where we now sat
      as if suspended in space..

Then upon a small, gentle slope of sand
we lay close together
as you read my new poems aloud.

Were you ever
  an emotional refugee
    in a directionless world?

You said,
    "A lot of your playtime
    is your imagination!"

I was conceived in love;
I was born ready for loving.
Society was not prepared
    for my individual freedom,
    nor was I prepared
    for its social restrictions.

Gentle are the outstretched hands
of love,
reaching out only to be acknowledged.

Why do people pin labels on themselves,
then run to find the group of people
the label represents?
Why?

TODAY...is the only day
you can live!

"It's easier for people
to look out a window,
than to look into a mirror,"
you said as we drove
down the city street.

When we first met, you told me,
> *"When I was younger I had a lot to give*
> *but I couldn't seem to find people*
> *who wanted it.*
> *Now you come into my life*
> *and want it all...*
> *I'm confused."*

As my feelings are born,
I feed them emotionally,
rather than allow them
to decay and die inside me.

Hurting goes away,
love never does.

People who do not love themselves
will not allow others to love them.
If I could bring forth your potential,
        your goodness,
                the quality of your loving,
then I know you would allow
        my love to penetrate
        the impregnable castle
        in which your true nature lives.
If I cannot get in,
then I will draw you out!

The quiet of your eyes
says all I need to know.

"God painted the earth for us,
and now we're erasing it,"
                you told me.

Come, my friend,
        let us journey to a new place,
        a place of your belonging,
        though it be unknown to you,
                believe in me.
Remove as much of the debris
        from your past as you can,
        making room for the happiness
        love's potential can restore.

I am so happy
     watching you discover yourself,
     having the freedom to express
     your feelings without reservation.
I love myself more
     for allowing that to happen.

We copy when we become bored;
we resist when we become afraid;
we create when we become stimulated;
we change when we become secure;
we love when we become loved.

You said,
"It seems as if every day I am offered something
but most of the time it is offered without
the person meaning or intending
to follow through."

Will you have faith
just one more time
that my words . . .
are sincere?

Fight for your right
      to be loved
as you would fight
      to obtain your freedom.

Most of us carry
      guilt feelings
which are born
in our childhood,
growing stronger
in our youth.

Now, you and I are working hard
      to discard this guilt
      by understanding
      not only the symptoms
         but the causes...
      and the cure.
Guilt is such a waste,
When it is imposed upon us
      by ignorance.

27

It's what's around me
that determines
      the beauty
within me.

28

Traditions,
the ages of history
and morality
may all be different,
but the human choices of loving
remain the same.

Most of my life I have searched,
taking the opportunity of situations,
trying to develop relationships
that could be built upon
for a lifetime.
I've traveled many different landscapes
and have been absorbed into many a city.
When I came to a dead end,
or detour,
or complications,
I always found a way to continue;
somewhere ahead,
I knew you would be there.

My friendship...
      is the best part of me.

You make me feel
    special,
        wanted,
            needed,
and you remember.

Sometimes when we take a shower together,
    washing each other's hair and body,
I feel like a child in a playground.
I enjoy playing with you.

You are very considerate
and observant of my feelings.
I sometimes wonder
    if my feelings are not also your own.
Time is teaching me . . .
    they are.

Hurts have taught me...
never give up loving,
be willing to take
another risk and chance...
otherwise tomorrow...
may be empty.

I have met and loved
*   many people who were different*
*   from the common and ordinary.*
But you are unique and special
*   among the different.*
It is because of that uniqueness
*   that I can make a promise to you,*
*   to live together and to harvest*
*   a special friendship.*

This evening by the fireplace,
lying naked on the fur rug beside you,
a dream of mine came true.

It's wonderful to have someone special
       to be concerned about.
Everywhere I go I look for things
       that will make you feel good.
Today it was a bouquet of flowers
       from a roadside stand
       and a quart of chocolate ice cream.
Yesterday I called you on the phone
       from the city just to say,
       "I love you."
Tomorrow just might be
       breakfast in bed.

Your childlike quality
is one of your best traits,
for it is filled with
        curiosity,
                excitement,
                        and frivolity.

*Friendship is
the foundation for
           being in love.*

This morning
     we shared the simple, uncluttered
     moments of living:
          reading poetry aloud,
          expressing our thoughts,
          daydreaming,
          and imagining ourselves
               in other worlds.
As we listened to music,
     carrying us into
     the magical ancient worlds of
     Greece and Rome,
our bodies merged together as
     one life-force.

I watched from the window
as you lay in the sun
near our river,
> *each moment tanning your body*
> *into the golden luster*
> *that gives a vitality and richness*
> *to the flesh and increases*
> *sensuality.*

"No one has ever taken the time
to love me as you have."
These words you spoke were hard to express,
for you were accepting my interpretation of
> *loving.*

My tears of happiness,
mingling with my life's blood,
are hidden from the eyes of others,
seen, in quiet understanding,
only by God.

Your whispers of passion and ecstasy
        in the night
deaden sounds within me,
of many a yesterday's sadness.

Your needs are mine
        to fulfill whenever I am able,
        never from obligation or pressure,
        but simply from my own personal desire.

Each and every day is filled with my caring for you.
        My giving is consistent,
    for in consistency I reveal
        my motives and intentions,
    my soul laying bare.

Your beauty enriches my life,
stimulating my creative ability
     beyond anything I have ever known.
Your body reflects the composition of nature.
How thrilling to look upon
     your magnificent nakedness,
     falling in love
          over and over again.

We have worked hard in creating
"a reality,
            a fantasy,
                        and a happiness
all rolled into one. . .
            a magic moment."

We slept together
             several times
      before we were united
      in sexual pleasure...
believing the first experience
to be more meaningful,
coming as it did
      from spontaneous feelings
rather than an expectant mind.

I am not your teacher.
I am only a reflection of who you are.

We can never give enough affection...
        the more we give,
        the more we need
                to give.
Thus we've helped each other...
                discover the happiness of
                touching.

Whenever we can
        we run out into Nature.
Even parks in the city
        satisfy our hunger
        for a natural environment.

Remember the day
        we spent at the park
        feeding the ducks and geese,
        playing frisbee and tennis
        and smiling at all the strangers...
I know our happiness was apparent
for the smiles were returned.

Our different abilities,
backgrounds
and personalities
are complements to the balance
of our relationship;—
from opposites we learn
to expand our knowledge,
understanding,
and interests.
I am comfortable with our differences
because I care to understand.
Loving you does that...
Loving myself does that.

I awoke this Fourth of July morning
            to your gentle kiss
and for the first time I heard
            the tender words
            "I love you,"
as I felt your breath
            against my lips.
Within myself, silent and unnoticed,
I exploded with joy.

            As our love grows
            we are finding
            a vast amount of interactions
            that make loving fun.
                        Tonight
            we did a crazy thing:
            As you were soaking in a bubblebath,
            we ate a midnight snack of strawberries
                        by candlelight.

Yesterday
> I found you.

Today
> I understand a part of myself.

Tomorrow
> We will explore together.

Your caring for me started from our first meeting
and has increased each and every day.
Not a day has gone by that you have not shown me
consideration and kindness,
even when you were tired or carried a burden
of your own.
You never cease to amaze me with your giving.

Many of the everyday chores that we share together
are done without playing roles
and without expecting the other
to complete the work that needs to be done
There is no drudgery in preparing meals,
      washing the clothes or dishes,
      cleaning the house,
      or running errands.
Because we love each other,
          it has become fun.

It's the little, everyday considerations
that make our relationship
healthy and vibrant.

Friends
don't become friends
until they enter
your heart.

I am a physical creature
          of the body's pleasures
          and promiscuous
          with my sensuality—
Yet I find
          satisfying your sensuality
          is a greater pleasure . . .
as you do the same for me.

I try never to take you for granted.
To someday say,
        "I wish I had. . ."
is a threatening sadness.

The more we are together
the more I am you
and the more you are me.
We are achieving
        a harmony in being different
        and being the same,
        without losing our
        individual natures.

We belong to no religion,
            organization, or label,
only to ourselves—
and a way of life
            that encompasses all
humankind.

We have often shared
        both pleasure and pain
while realizing all
        the aspects of loving.

My beloved...
        may I share in teaching you
        what you can do with your
        new-found freedom?

When I first met you
I felt I had known you
for a long time.
Your words did not challenge my beliefs
and your affection was
innocent of deceit.

Very often your body says more than your words.
This morning
we lay in bed making love,
slowly,
intensely,
passionately,
without restraint,
without the pressure of having to get up
to commitments and responsibilities
of the day.
We always seem to take the time for each other.

Making you happy
*   makes me happy.*
It is so simple...
*   love, I mean.*

The more I observe you,
even without your knowing it,
the more I can put together
the parts and pieces
that comprise your personality
and understand your struggles.

The brilliant, sunny hours
        never prevent our caressing each other
tenderly.
        We move swiftly away
        from tradition
when we share affection,
                even making love
        has no specific roots
                in conformity
                or a particular place.
We are spontaneous in making love...
        There are many romantic places
besides the bedroom.

I have learned from you:
                For one to speak with authority
                on the subject of love
        is a fool's lament.
When you live love
        you are an authority
                without words.

As we were driving home,
God blessed our love by giving us
    nine different rainbows
stretching for over a hundred miles
    in the Willamette Valley of Oregon.
The last rainbow fell upon our home...
Was this a simple miracle?
            God's message to us?

Occasionally I see an urgency
in your eyes,
telling me you are running
toward loving,
not away from it.

With you I feel whole.
All my feelings and emotions
are magnified a hundred times,
to such an extent
that my natural highs and lows
have greatly enlarged
the scale of my being.

Never in my life
have I felt these feelings
which are stimulated by you.
Each day my emotions are amplified.
Is there no end to this magic of my being?

We both are idealistic
and if given the opportunity
we will find romance
around every corner.
Our imagination is never ending,
believing anything possible.

I would rather have a friend to love
than to be in love
without the friend.

74

I never have to perform for you
to gain your love or acceptance,
because honesty eliminates
the word games.

Riches
can accent our lives
rather than dominate them.

*The only schedule that I keep in my life
is made up of the promises
that I make.*

I've held you
            a thousand times
in my fantasies.
                    Now that you are real
I can hold you in my arms.

We sat by the river
            as the sun fell behind the trees.
We didn't need words
            to express our feelings,
Just our arms around each other.

I love
            the way
you love me.

So often I have posed questions to you,
guiding your understanding.
Even when it hurt you,
you became clearer in the awareness of yourself.

We had been together a while
when I found these words scribbled
on a torn piece of paper on your dresser:
"Sitting here
I am trying to write my feelings—
then realizing that many times
I had stopped myself from feeling,
and us from growing."

With us:
>*Innocence is an attitude*
>*not just*
>*the absence of experience.*

Watching you from across the room
            as you read a magazine,
creates a glow inside me.
Just having you near,
            in the same house,
is comforting.

Disappointments have arisen
            in our relationship,
            either from hopes
            that went unfulfilled
            or expectations
            that were shattered,
yet our loving repairs the damage
created by emotional storms
            or thought disasters.

We both assert our personality through
            words and actions, confirming,
"This is me!"

Sitting in the movie theater
we laughed and felt joy in watching
the innocence,
the uncertainty,
the clumsiness of two youths
growing in their first experiences of loving.
The movie ending, a surprise tragedy,
opened old wounds within our lives.
We wept in silent understanding,
not wanting to be reproached
for our feelings.
Driving home I asked if you had ever wished
to recapture your innocence!

Living for you,
not just myself,
is now a reason...

It is a good feeling to leave home
early in the morning,
alone for the city,
knowing you'll be here
when I return
in the evening.
It is good to have someone to come home to,
but it is paradise
to have that someone
to make love to.

Often we have had long conversations
concerning our feelings,
always expanding our awareness
of each other.
We've never argued,
or battled,
or demanded understanding.
We have debated and discussed,
growing to enjoy
these encounters.

Last night we were separated by our needs.
I felt the need to share sexual pleasure;
in your uncertainty
you wanted to find peace in going to sleep.
Being close to you in bed,
I couldn't sleep
for my need extended throughout the night.
In the morning we discussed our differences...
We became closer in understanding.

Such tremendous joy
I have received from what is natural!
During the absence of human companionship,
Nature was always there.

Loving seems to bring forth answers
that otherwise are lost
in the confusion
not loving creates.

As long as we can openly discuss
our misunderstandings,
our disagreements,
there will never be a need for
substitutes
or escape routes from
our relationship.

Your thoughts reveal
　　　　what you can be.
Your words reveal
　　　　what you want to be.
Your actions reveal
　　　　who you are.

Some days are surely better than others.
On a day when I felt depressed,
you whispered in my ear,
　　　　"For every tear
　　　　there will be a day of smiling."
I hugged you.

God sees what we do,
　　　　not what we think.

Before you left you asked me
for a photo
to carry with you.
I wonder if you'll remember to look at it.
Maybe your mind is too preoccupied with
your returning.

Sometimes you need to be alone with your thoughts.
Sometimes you need to spend the day
     doing things just for yourself.
Sometimes we need to be separated by days
     so we never take each other's
     love for granted.

Please come home soon.
I got used to sleeping close to you
and now I am uncomfortable and restless
as I learn to sleep alone, once again.

Even though you'll only be gone ten days,
each day without you grows
                longer and longer.
You have become a part of my life.
Come home early
                if you can
and surprise me.

The sadness of your leaving
                was replaced by
the joy of your returning.

96

Today we found a hidden valley
in a remote section of southern Arizona.
As we took the time
to explore this wonder of nature
We became aware that this was
"A Valley of Perfect Balance."
If only people could find this valley
within themselves, and explore,
as we did.

We made this day
     different from routine
by cooking a special dinner
and eating by candlelight on the patio.
It took extra time and energy
but then isn't that what love is all about?

I don't want to love like everyone else—
     they're limited.
I am so happy that I am able to share myself
     the way I do.

I have speculated many times in my life...
            what it would be like
            to share the intimacy of lovers.
Never in my wildest dreams or imaginations
            could it measure up to this reality
            I have found.
It is like seeing a sunset
            that has been condensed into
            a tiny photograph,
            then one day later
        experiencing the real thing.

New experiences to us
        were intricate parts of our relationship,
        leading to all sorts of discoveries—
"Knowledge without experience
        is a human being who has not yet learned."

Once you asked me,
    "When signing your name
    do you honestly know the person
    you're writing about?"

When you know there is someone loving you,
each day bursts forth anew.

Once you were adrift
    on windless seas
    of loneliness;
then your sails began to fill
    with the winds of sharing.
Now your course carries you
    to the harbor
        of friends. . .
            and lovers.

Answers make us intelligent,
but questions make us human. . .
          what was it you asked me?

    Mistrust is so exhausting.

       Sometimes your love
            clutches me so hard
            I feel I am strangling.
       When you notice
            you shyly let go.

With you
I express my love
    through the three forms of communication
       each of us possesses:

My body   sensuality and sexuality

My mind   intellect

My emotions   outward manifestation of my feelings.

    These are expressed
without reservations and without any
restrictions.

    With others
I may love, I do not give all of myself
    and I may only express myself
        to various degrees
        in these forms of communication.
        With those I like
I give less of myself.
    You. . .
have all of me.

I gaze at our river
          while overhead
the raindrops bounce gently off the leaves,
disappearing into the earth beneath my feet.
Everywhere out here
I feel your presence in all that is
          natural and pleasing.

The simpler love is
the longer it will last.

I feel so good
            collecting memories
      with the same person
      through all the seasons.

      How often I have seen
      people abandon their feelings...
                  Remember!

You asked me,
        early one morning,
      "Why do we fear to be naked
      in mind, body, and soul
      with others? Is it because
      we fear to be naked with
              ourselves?"

      Many people boast of loving,
      but few fill their commitments.
      You are becoming one of the very few.

Your words always express
what is in your heart:
"Those who have the eyes
to behold beauty,
know the first secret of love."

Our journey in life
*   is one in which the search*
*   is for ourselves.*
I now have a companion.

It has not been the amount
*   we give to each other*
but the quality of
*   our giving*
that has become our truth.

You make love with your eyes,
*   and your smile,*
*   and your words,*
*   and your hands,*
not like many people who only make love
*   with their sex organs!*

One evening as I sat in the living room
          working on my poetry,
you handed me a piece of paper with these words:
"This is my way of saying,
          'Thank you,'
for knowing that inside me
there was a better person
than I ever realized
and for helping me to find that person
          through your caring."

"To love me is to squeeze
          every ounce of loving out of me"—
these words you spoke
          as the night brought passion
into our lives.

Your love softens
the burden of my responsibilities
                    and commitments.

At different times
we have made promises to each other,
meaning to fulfill them;
but there is a tendency
to allow time to subdue the feeling
        belonging to the promises—
if we let it.

As I write these words
            my eyes are filled with tears,
        not from sorrow,
but from a kind of happiness
I have never known till now.

Sometimes you need to be understood
*   rather than to understand;*
Sometimes you desire to be shown affection
*   without reciprocating;*
Sometimes you become fatigued
*   and rely on your friends' energy;*
Sometimes your needs are silent
*   but your companion hears them*
*   more each day!*

We are both rich in feelings,
often susceptible to the hurts and repression
*   inflicted by social attitudes.*
Because we have each other for support,
our vulnerability is an asset
in holding us together.

Even with you, my love,
loneliness sometimes surges to the surface
of my thoughts.
My heart and pulse beat rapidly
from the pains of the past.
When it is all over
I am grateful there is you.

We have discovered that we directly
fulfill our needs,
wants,
and desires by making things happen
rather than by waiting in silence,
skimming over life and
relationships.

*I hope that some day
all human beings will find
their own freedom...*
        as we have found ours.

Because you are my special person,
I give to you more of myself
than anyone else.

We have both made commitments to stay together
for the rest of our lives.
But if during that time
either one of us becomes a stranger to the other,
our commitments were not made to the strangers
we might become—
We are free to separate,
still loving one another.

Perhaps, one day, our society will be composed of
                    lovers
                    and
                    friends to love
whose devotion will be in tune with Nature
and all that is natural.

    As our relationship becomes secure and stable,
    then sharing love with others
    will not become a threat. . .
    but an extension of our love.

We once said hello
and it all began...
But we shall never say goodbye...

For goodbyes
are too final.

These two pages are for you to write upon...
   Let it become your magic moment!

Please feel free to write me of your feelings and comments concerning this book:

Walter Rinder
c/o Celestial Arts
231 Adrian Road
Millbrae, CA 94030

WALT RINDER